BRITISH TO AMERICAN ENGLISH

A DICTIONARY AND GUIDE TO THE ENGLISH LANGUAGE

BY

Hi ESL

TABLE OF CONTENTS

Introduction

The words British, Brit or Briton refer to natives of the United Kingdom. They may be from Scotland, Wales, England or Ireland. In this book we use the words interchangeably. Now and then we refer to the English (not the language but the people) or the Englishman. Then we mean someone particularly from England. The Americans are natives of the US, the States or the United States and they speak a dialect of English we will call US English. It is interesting how divergent the two dialects can be as we explore in the next few pages. First we go on a guided trip back in time to the formation of English, and then through its evolution on both sides of the Atlantic. Then we take a fleeting look at the cultural differences of the two nations and their customs. Included is a helpful guide to some common idioms that are completely different in the two dialects. Also, you will find a glossary of common words that mean something completely different over the water. The spelling can also be quite different so near the end you will find a spelling guide.

Preface

A road has been excavated from out of Middlesborough that winds through the Lake District to the sea at Kent and washes out into the Atlantic. But in the history of England all roads lead to London. This one doesn't. The reason is that when it was built London wasn't important. The year was 827AD. At that time England was ruled by a king, but not one who spoke any English. At that time, English did not exist. Britons had become Britons by migrating from Wales, Cornwall and Central mainland Europe to the isle. They were Celts and spoke Celtic.

Then, the Romans invaded the isle in 43AD and by 50AD built a city on the isthmus between the Thames and the Atlantic opening a center of commerce and trade to the European mainland. The Roman province of Britannia was Latin.

Within four centuries Anglo-Saxons invaded Britannia. The Germans took over. Some suggest they unleashed a massacre on the Celtic-Roman population and effectively wiped them out. This might be true but at any rate, after 449AD the Roman never again recaptured Britannia after it was lost.

The Anglo-Saxons were a mix from all over Europe whose native languages influenced the Germanic tongue they held in common. And they settled on the isle until interrupted by the Vikings from Northern Europe. About 1% of the English we speak is squarely derived from

Norse. Then in 1066 the Normans who felt entitled to succeed King Edward the Confessor who had just died, invaded. The Normans were from Normandy where French was spoken. Right now, more than half of English is derived from French. That the French were the ruling class and the Anglo-Saxons were the working class can be seen in the words for beef (French: boeuf), mutton (French: mouton), pork (French: porque) being meat on the table as served to the elite able to afford meat. But the Saxon words cow, sheep and pig are the live versions, because the Saxons were the herders of the livestock.

The Hundred Years war began in 1337 and as the ruling class declined in strength, the use and importance of French declined. A mixture of Anglo-Saxon, French and Germanic languages from the native Britons starts to become English. During those years Geoffrey Chaucer chooses to write a history of his land not in French, nor in Latin (the languages of the literate), but in a strange new language with none of the prestige or security of those languages. It was a chance for Chaucer to take. How would anyone be able to read his work a century or two later when no one spoke English anymore? French and Latin were the language of the educated. The Plantagenet king of England himself scarcely knew English. The Bible, the central text of European culture of that time, was in those languages. Who knew whether this upstart creole would be around in a few generations? Chaucer may have considered the risk of writing such an expansive work as the Canterbury Tales in so transient a language as English. But the bet paid off handsomely. Not many years after he started it in 1343, John Wycliffe began to translate the Bible into this new language from Latin.

In Germany, Gutenberg had perfected his press and shipped it to England and throughout Europe. And so the stage was set for a new era of knowledge, exploration and discovery. The loosing of the grip of the clergy and the availability of the Bible and other literature thanks to the lower cost of printing meant that intellectuals, statesmen, merchants and travellers all over Europe could meet each other and share ideas. So it was that English again drew influence from French, but also Greek, Italian, Spanish and other languages. New territories were being discovered. Much like today India and China were the production houses for goods the European market were prepared to pay for and trade routes crisscrossed the globe. Africa and the Americas were discovered. The opportunities for commerce were suddenly immense. Slaves were kidnapped and delivered as free labour for the booming economy of Europe. The British navy decimated the naval powers of Spain, Netherlands and France. So rose the Anglo world power and the Empire that now included the vast new North America, Africa, India and Australia. This Empire covered the globe, 1 in 4 humans were subject to it. And as the colonies sprawled continents, imported natives from the subjugated lands brought their Oriental and Occidental languages to Britain and more exotic linguistic influences were felt.

The British colonies spread all across the globe. Of these colonies were "The Americas". What are now Canada and the United States were colonies of the Empire until the late 1700s. Their language was largely imported by colonial power and education. But the politics of America was very different to Britain. It governed itself. It rejected the rulership of an elite aristocratic class in favour of a republican model where the citizens had the vote. There was an unpleasant fight over tea imports taxed by the colonists off the coast of Massachussetts and so began a fight that divided America from the British Empire.

And so George Bernard Shaw could rightly call England and America 'two countries divided by a common language'. The English pilgrims migrated west and settled across a vast landscape. They farmed. They eventually built factories. They very reluctantly joined WWI in the last minute. From that point forward the world domination was shared by a dual power - England and America - the Anglo-American world power. America attracted immigrants from all over the globe. They made money. Their stock market crashed. The Great Depression hit. Then after WWII, which devastated mainland Europe and much of the United Kingdom, the United States emerged as an enforcer of might or right for the rest of the world. It exercised a different brand of domination. America exported its culture across the earth through radio, television and more recently the Internet.

The geography, social structure, political and ideological persuasion of the people and the sheer variety of their origins have left their marks on the language now spoken in America. There are now, perhaps irreconcilable differences between their language and the language of the Crown.

What are some of those differences? How can you navigate them successfully? This is the curiosity we turn our hand to explore.

Which is English?

Is it spoken by the Queen and the Royal family? Only 2% of Britons use that hyperlect. Is it the common language of Britain? There scarcely is a common language in Britain as it varies tremendously between Wales, Scotland, North England, Ireland and dramatically within those regions as well. Is it the language spoken in America, a renegade of her Majesty's Empire? They speak very differently from the English. Then you have Australia, South Africa and the non-English speaking Commonwealth who all speak completely variant English dialects of their own.

My conclusion is that, thanks in great part to what was once the British Empire, ours is the common language of the world with many differences. The native English speaker communicates, not in "English" in the pure sense but, in one of its many dialects.

This was the hard experience of Maurice, a Swiss Frenchman on holiday with an English family in South Africa. He was well armed, he believed, with a French-English dictionary as Plan B when his ever-faltering English deserted him altogether. As the holiday continued his English improved little and the dictionary fell further into disuse. His fellow travellers didn't understand his translations. Here are some of the expression that got Maurice all unstuck.

The US dictionary gave "gas" as the word for petrol. For the British "gas" could be a fart, a cylinder of LPG (liquid petroleum gas), a vapour of any substance but petrol would not likely come to mind. After all, petrol is mostly liquid when its pumped into the tank. He pointed at buskers along the roadside and was keen to take pictures of them. They had just slipped out of view when he called to look at the . . . He grabbed the dictionary and found the expression "sidewalk". No one in sight was walking sideways. The buskers were back in view and everyone corrected him, "pavement". He asked if anyone was going to the . . . "drugstore". The car stopped in front of a shop and the answer was no. Of course this was a "drugstore" or just an ordinary "store" but his fellow tourists didn't know what he meant. He looked with frustration at his dictionary and started to think better of using it.

Of course since plenty of television streams across both sides of the Atlantic and work pulls people across it to, Americans have the chance of hearing British English and vice-versa. Total ignorance of each other's dialect is not common.

But, although over 300 languages are spoken in the US, only in the last decade has the American government declared English to be the official language. Before that America had no official language.

Let's take a look then at the cultural differences so strongly entrenching the use of English in these two nations.

Cultural differences between the Americans and the British

No Brit is completely British and no American is completely and quintessentially American. People are people, each with their own idiosyncrasies. At the risk of making wild generalisations, let us attempt to summarise a set of contrasts between the typically British vs the typically American experience.

When in Britain:

Making small talk

Small talk will invariably include discussing the weather. The weather is a real topic for conversation. British weather is generally dreadful and talking about it reminds everyone of how intolerable and unpleasant it really is. Apparently the British feel it's important to keep reminding one another of that fact. It's a peculiarity of Britons not shared by other cultures.

Getting around

British roads and cars are very much smaller than American cars. Many drive manual hatchbacks on the road. The SUV to a Brit may just as well be a 4x4. They drive on the left side of the road. Usually changing gears with what the American will call a "stick-shift".

It is just not done to make small talk with strangers on public transport. When you get into a bus or taxi you mind your own business until it is time to get out.

The Accent to the British

No matter how rich or poor you are in Britain your accent defines you. Accents may reveal residential address, educational background, ancestral prestige and any number of other important details to the Englishman that no one else will pick up on or think of as important. Most people just look at your dress, shoes, cellphone, hairstyle or wristwatch. The Englishman will listen to your accent.

Tea break

In most households you will be offered tea frequently and at random throughout the day. Tea is much preferred to coffee. In Britain the tea is superb but coffee is not important. People have no problem even keeping instant coffee in their homes, just as a gesture really.

Table manners

On a date, almost of more importance than anything else, is table manners. No matter how pleasant, genuine and charming you are, a second date will likely depend more on whether you ate neatly and appropriately. Yes, table manners in Britain really do matter that much.

Schools and Uniforms

Boys schools are attended by only boys and they all wear uniforms in Britain. Girls schools are only for girls and they all wear school uniforms likewise. The idea of youngsters attending school in civilian clothing is not favoured in Britain. Might it not breed disrespect and counter the disciplined culture of learning?

Toasting

The British might say "cheers" to a toast and at the end of an evening, they will definitely say "cheers" to mean goodbye. To an American "cheers" is confusing and might mean anything. There are plenty of words that mean many things in Britain and nothing in America, and vice-versa. More about that later, though.

Gun control

No guns are carried around by private citizens in Britain. Arms are in the hands of the Crown. This is just how the social order of Britain is maintained, and it certainly is maintained.

The effects of slave trade history are seen and felt in the United States more acutely than in the United Kingdom. But far less racism seems to exist in Britain as very few slaves were in slavery there. Even throughout the colonies, slavery ended long before it did in America.

Almost everyone in Britain has a washing machine but tumble driers are rare. In America they are mandatory.

Pubs and privacy

The word 'pub' is short for "public house". It may be disappointing to the American but in Britain, pubs are really just public houses. They serve more as community living rooms for catching up with old friends and chatting than taverns for consuming alcohol.

Britons value privacy highly. They appear very guarded, even aloof to begin with. After several interactions they may thaw a little but the first contact is not especially friendly or warm. If you are invited, come punctually and please leave at an appropriate hour (read, not later than 11pm). It would be grossly rude to overstay or just pop in without an invitation or at the very least advanced warning.

Assertiveness and passive-aggression

Assertiveness about personal preferences is not regarded as mannerly in Britain. If one wants to say something it should be valid and factually-based. It is best to be quiet until one has something to say that really needs to be said. But on the other hand, the British feel free to say things they absolutely do not mean like the waiter and patron at a restaurant who exchange the requisite "Thank you" and "Have a good day" at the end of a meal. There is not a wisp of good will or sincerity in that exchange but its obligatory and no one wants to disappoint.

Corporate culture

British companies take far more paid leave than American firms do. Annually Britons get and take 28 days paid leave. In America they may be entitled to 16 days but averagely no one takes more than half of that off each year.

In the British world of work, employment laws tend towards favouring the employee. The American economy was built more on American soil by entrepreneurial spirit and assertiveness. The British system is comparatively more bureaucratic and hierarchical than the American one.

When in America:

Starting the conversation

With the exception of the really big cities it's fine to start a conversation with a complete stranger in America. On public transport, waiting in a queue or anywhere where you interface with other people small talk is just a charming and friendly thing to get into. In Britain it is impertinent.

Getting around

Cars are big in the States. Bonnets, oh sorry I mean, hoods are huge and gleaming. They guzzle "gas", yes "fuel" rapaciously. They drive on straight, flat, wide roads for miles and miles and sometimes many days. The British isles cover a very small landmass so cross country journeys are different.

Your Accent in America

No one cares how you "talk", I mean "speak". It just matters that they understand you and they feel that you mean what you say. Of course your clothes, shoes, laptop, phone and pen matter. Of course they are checking the car you arrived in, whether you own or rent your home, where you live and which tax bracket you are in. Those things matter a lot more than how you pronounce your consonants.

Coffee, anyone?

At a restaurant, or in a private home, coffee and soda are standard available drinks. In restaurants in the States refills to either are poured thick and fast. Tea is not nearly as interesting to the American. Maybe they really want that caffeine kick?

Call me Al

Depending on the culture of the people you are dealing with it is generally best to call people by their first names in America. It is not wrong to say Mr. or Ms. but it sounds very formal. The English may not appreciate that. They may view it as overfamiliarity but the Americans are just generally more casual and relaxed in their culture.

In America "everything is awesome" so get used to it.

Americans talk loudly and freely about everything and anything. They feel no compunction about airing personal views no one else shares. They say what they think, when it comes to mind. They are more confident and assertive in their communication styles than the British who won't tolerate self-exaltation and boastfulness. Speaking with a lot of enthusiasm is "awesome" in the States. It means you are obviously really "into it", you mean it and you feel passionately about what you are saying. In Britain it would completely detract from the valid message you are trying to bring across to add too much fervour or emotion to your speech.

Working in America

Time really is treated like money in American working culture. Punctuality is very important. It is better to be a little early than on-time. In Britain, on time it just right.

What is considered polite in the UK may be very rude in the US and the other way around. Let's see some differences.

Customs and Etiquette

When in Britain

Go to a restaurant

Waiters will welcome you, seat you and attend to you in Britain but they are formal and different to the American ones. Don't expect them to be chatty and friendly, always at the ready to take more orders or refill your soda. If you want to drink another Coke, you would need to order another Coke. The British waiter may leave you alone for hours at the table. If you want something else you could call for them. But, they won't be asking you many questions beyond "What will you be having?"

Don't be too picky in a British restaurant. If it is not on the menu it would be impolite to ask for it. If you ask for too many omissions or substitutions, the British waiter and the kitchen behind him will get annoyed. In America you can usually get away with this. In Britain that approach to a menu card will not win you any friends.

A visitor to Britain should just be aware that water is not free. It comes in a bottle from the manufacturer and must be paid for. If you ask for tap water you will be considered cheap or miserly so rather don't do that.

In Britain, double check that you have asked for the bill. They won't bring it to you unless you ask. Asking for the bill is your signal that for you the meal and the visit to the restaurant is concluding.

Beforehand, tell the waiter if you plan to split the bill so that he can prepare separate receipts for each of you. He will likely be unhappy to do this after the bill has rung up. If you decide or speak up about splitting the bill when it's time to pay, you will need to do the tally yourself.

In the UK the tip is 10% of the bill unless you were really dissatisfied with the service. It would be excusable if you choose not to tip because you really didn't like the service. It is absolutely no okay to refer to "he" or "she" when that person is standing in the room with them. The reaction (the first time) will be shock, outrage and disbelief.

The British waiter is insulting you when he says "Have a pleasant afternoon" especially before he takes your order - you've been evicted and you need to understand that.

The waiter may ask you what you want in UK but in US he might ask you what you do, where you are from and what your star sign is. Deeply inappropriate to a Brit.

Go to a business meeting:

The American has no problem promoting himself. The Brit finds that objectionable and unprofessional. You will be mocked and brought right back down from that self-exalted perch. The boss wants only facts, clear, bullet-pointed and unexaggerated. Do not get emotional in the British workplace. Tone enthusiasm down a lot. Do not express your own opinion enthusiastically. In US that would be a good thing though.

A great job would be complimented as "not bad". In America, it would be "so phenomenal".

Visit someone in their home:

In Britain the front door to a home stays closed. Your house is your castle. People don't just pop in. If you do have the invitation to just pop in, call ahead to be sure your hosts are home and ready to receive you. When you enter, take off your hat. Especially for men it would be very rude to wear a hat in the house. When someone says "How do you do?" this is not a question. Reply with "How do you do?"

It would be unusual and embarrassing to embrace or kiss in greeting. Prolonged eye contact makes everyone feel uncomfortable. Introduce the junior to the senior and not the other way around in Britain.

Britons are not especially noted for their spontaneity, warmth and friendliness. They might warm up, (read thaw out) slowly. They can and do form very deep friendships though. It may take some work to build a rapport so patience is needed.

The traditionally stiff upper lip has relaxed over the generations but the British aren't share their hearts and minds with over familiarity just yet.

Eat dinner:

At the dinner table you will find a fork on the left of your plate and a knife on the right. Sometimes you will find a few sets of cutlery with minor differences in shape and size on either side of your plate. When Britons sit down to eat at the dinner table they use knives and forks to eat everything. This is strange to the Americans who don't use cutlery, or if they do they may only use a fork.

If a napkin is on the table in Britain, please use it before and not after the meal. When the waiter says "what would you like?" Feel free to say "please" several times in your response. And afterwards, say "thank you" liberally.

Get around town:

As a pedestrian on British pavements jaywalking is fine and everyone does it. But the Brits will wait very patiently at the zebra crossing if there is one until such time as the traffic lights change and they are allowed to go.

If you find yourself on public transport, try not to give in to the urge to speak to anyone. People do not talk to complete strangers on public transport, that is taboo.

The Americans may struggle with the British manual hatchbacks on the comparatively tiny roads driving on the left side, not the right. England is smaller than America so space, distance and time feels different to them. The British police smile more and tend to go about in male, female pairs.

When in America:

Go to a restaurant

In America you can feel free to speak about any personal preferences. If you want a tomato salad with cucumber instead of tomato the chef might roll his eyes but he will put it together for you. In the UK you would do better to keep quiet unless the food really is inedible.

The American waiter is smiling, frequently comes back to check that everything is going well and takes any additional orders for food or drinks efficiently. They are also chatty, they might ask you where you work, how your day was, maybe even what your star sign is. The Englishman would be alarmed and annoyed by that. That's just part of really super service in the States.

After you have stopped ordering food the American waiter will bring the bill to you. It will arrive on your table without you asking for it. This doesn't mean that they are chasing you out of the restaurant. Gratuity in America is ordinarily a tip 15-20% of the bill. These tips are the only income the waiters get. In most States waiters manage to sustain an average income that is far below the minimum wage. The tip is comparatively higher than in the UK and it's mandatory but on the other hand the service is much better.

Go to a business meeting

In America punctuality and deadlines are really important. Missing a deadline is seen as blatantly irresponsible. The American worker is typically a very hard-worker, putting in no less than 40 hours a week all year, with very little paid leave. Getting really emotional and enthusiastic about your opinion or proposal is a great thing in America, not so Britain. The Americans take enthusiasm as sincerity, so they believe you mean what you say when you say it with passion.

Visit someone in their home

When invited to someone's home bring a small gift for the host/hostess. Chocolates, flowers or a good bottle of wine are usually appropriate. If you can find a valid reason to compliment the food, do that. If you can't then rather say less.

In Britain people say please a lot. In America the "please" is inferred more often by the tone of voice and not spoken out loud. The Brits might view this as rude but it is not meant rudely.

Americans will call their offspring "kids" and in Britain it would sound like they are being referred to as 'little goats' and it sounds rude. Britons would say "children" which sounds more treasured.

A brat is not a good thing in America, it's perfectly okay to call someone you have just met a 'brat' in Britain. In the States, it is best not to overstay when invited over to someone's house. Generally Americans socialise earlier and the parties end earlier than in Britain. Brits on the other hand have been keeping late hours for centuries and show no signs of quitting.

Please avoid the topics of religion, politics, criticisms of the government, racism, abortion and how much money your hosts make.

Kissing others of the same gender might be controversial in America. Hugs are for close friends and family. A firm handshake is enough of a greeting and maintains the integrity of your acquaintances personal space.

Eat

Americans don't like using knives at the table. It can be difficult cutting up food with the side of a fork in your right hand but average Americans tend to rise to the challenge. Some do cut their food up with a knife first, but then they promptly abandon the knife and continue the rest of the meal armed with only a fork.

They don't have the same relationship with the dinner table that is common in Europe. Their waiters are always sharp and at the ready to exceed customer expectations and that is the standard of customer care that Americans expect.

At home the food is passed around the circle so each can take his share of food. When you are done, it's fine to show it by leaving a small amount of food on your plate and putting the fork, or whichever cutlery was used, at the side of the plate.

Americans don't use finger bowls. Traditionally, the Americans could not afford them. You might find finger bowls at very posh restaurants but not on the average dinner table. In Europe they are not very common but still seen.

Get around town

Jaywalking is a crime in America. One may freely hail a taxi by walking out onto the street but it is illegal to cross the street unless you do so at the designated place at the green pedestrian traffic light. The police may be around on foot or horseback in a large American city. When walking on the sidewalk it is polite to stay in single file with your group so others can walk freely in the opposite direction.

A-Z Guide to British Idioms

A	angry as-is - warts and all argument - kerfuffle	do one's nut Steaming	I was angry. Did me nut. He is still angry. He's still steaming.
	as-is	warts and all	I'll have it warts and all. I'll take it as it is.
	argument	kerfuffle	What was that kerfuffle? Why was there an argument/tiff over differing views?
B	bad	pant's	That's pants. That's bad.
	broke	skint quids in	I'm totally skint. I am totally broke. He's quids in. He has no money
	busybody (nosy neighbour)	curtain twitcher	She's such a curtain twitcher. She is such a busybody
C	call (phone)	give me a bell, tinkle, ring	Just give me a ring. Just give me a phone call.
	caught (caught in the act/red-handed)	bang to rights	It's bang to rights there mate. You've been caught my friend.
	crazy	barmy, crackers	Chap's barmy. The man is crazy.
	convict or ex-convict	lag	Never came 'round the old lag. He never got his life back on track after his release from prison.
	confused	lost the plot	They lost the plot with that series. They wrote the series in a confusing way.
	coward	girl's blouse	Don't be a big girl's blouse. Don't be a coward.
	cold	parky	It's parky out. It's cold outside.
D	discovered - got wise to it - found out;	got wise to it, got found out	Me mum got wise to it. My mother discovered it. Your car got found out. Your car was discovered to be (usually overrated).
	dishonest	bent as a nine-bob note	I wouldn't, the bloke's bent as a nine-bob note. I would not get involved. This man is corrupt/dishonest.
	drunk	hammered, bladdered, steaming, plastered	Let's get plastered. Let's get completely drunk.

	disrupt	throw a spanner in the works	Not meaning to throw a spanner in the works, but … I don't mean to disrupt things, but …
E	blinding	excellent	Blinding good job, mate. That was an excellent job my friend.
F	fart	pop, puff a dart	Did you just pop? Did you just puff a dart? Did you just fart?
	food	tucker	That's some pucker tucker. That's really good food.
G	geek - anorak	anorak	In her room all day, she's such an anorak. She spends all day in her room, she's such a geek.
	gossip (chat)	chinwag	Pop in for a chinwag? Would you like to come over for a chat?
H	happy	pleased as pie	He looked pleased as pie a moment ago. He looked very happy a moment ago.
I	idiot (fool, inept person)	git, plonker, ponce, sod, tosser	Utter sod! Tosser! Git! Idiot!
J			
K	conk	serious breakdown	Conked in for good. It is seriously broken down and can't be fixed.
L	lush -	a frequent drinker of alcohol (not necessarily an alcoholic)	Lolly's a lush a bit. Lolly drinks frequently.
M	miserable	mardy bum	He's a moany mardy bum. He is a miserable complainer.
	messed up	bodged it	He bodged it. He did a very bad job.
N	nonsense	tosh, bollocks, poppycock	What tosh! Bollocks! Poppycock! Nonsense!
	nothing	Sweet Fanny Adams	What'd you up to? Sweet Fanny Adams. What are you doing? Nothing.
	nice	the mutts nuts, the bees knees, pucker	She was just a bucket of bees knees. She was just very nice. This spot's just the mutt's nuts. This is a very nice place. Pucker place you got. You have a very nice place.
O	outstanding	corker	Max was corker. Max did an outstanding job.
P	pleased	chuffed	Right chuffed with yourself, you are. You are very pleased with yourself.
	police	fuzz, Old Bill, bobby, rozzer, PC plod	Gotta dash, Old Bill will be along in a minute. I must go, the police will be here shortly.
	procrastinating	fannying about	Stop fannying about! Stop procrastinating!

		punch	paste	I'll paste your face. I'll punch you in the face.
Q	Quiet	belt up	Belt up! Be quiet!
R	Rude	gobby, lippy, mouthy,	Don't get gobby now! Don't be rude!
S	stupid	two bricks short of a load; lift doesn't get to the top floor; two sandwiches short of a picnic	That blokes two bricks short of a load. That man is stupid.
	steal	filch	Got a feeling the old misers filching me. I suspect the old miser is steal from me/cheating me.
	self-exalting	all mouth, no trousers	He's all mouth, no trousers. He is all talk and no action.
T	Tabloid (cheap sensationalist magazine)	penny-dreadful	Flipped through the penny-dreadful. What bollocks! I paged through the cheap sensationalist magazine. What nonsense!
	Temper tantrum	paddy	Done with your paddy? Is your temper tantrum over?
	Toilet	bog, johns, loo	I'm off to the loo. I'm going to the toilet.
	Toilet paper	bog roll	They run the bog roll so stock up. They use a lot of toilet paper keep that in stock.
	Traffic patrolwoman	lollipop lady	You're a lollipop lady? You are a traffic patrolwoman?
	Truant (feigning illness to get out of work)	skive off, toss off	You tossing off again? Are you feigning illness to get out of work/school? Are you playing truant?
	Thanks	Ta!	Ta very much! Thank you very much!
U	upset	knickers in a knot	No need to get your knickers in a knot. You don't need to get upset.
	unpleasant	grotty	Grotty outfit that is. That is a nasty, unpleasant place.
	urinate	spend a penny, going for a jimmy	I'm off to spend a penny. I'm going to the men's toilet.
V	valueless thing	groat	You owe me a groat. You owe me nothing.
W			
X			
Y			
Z			

A-Z Guide to American Idioms

A	annoyed	miffed	You don't want to see her miffed. You don't want to see it when she gets annoyed.
	athlete	jock	High-school jocks line up for that stuff. Athletic high schoolers really like that.
	admirable	big	That's so big of you. You did a very admirable thing.
	barely	skin of one's teeth	She got through by the skin of her teeth. She barely succeeded.
B	binge	pig out	It's raw pigging out like that. It's unpleasant binge eating like that.
C	car	wheels	Don't have wheels today. I don't have transport (my car) today.
	caught	busted	They were busted. They were caught.
	chat	shoot the breeze	We shot the breeze over drinks. We chatted and enjoyed drinks together.
	co-drivers seat	shotgun	I'll ride shotgun. I'll sit in the co-driver's seat. Or as an idiom it means 'I'll be second in command.'
	cool	sick	One sick party. A very cool party.
	crazy	screwball	The screwball duo of comedy are coming. The crazy comic duo are coming.
	criticise (especially in hindsight, after the work is complete)	Monday morning quarterback	Don't be the Monday morning quarterback. Don't criticise how we did it.
D	drunk	juiced up	He got juiced up and bailed. He got drunk and left.
	disaster	wipeout, fail	After the wipeout of yesterday, I wonder what is going through his mind. After yesterday's disaster, I wonder what he is thinking.
	divulge (especially a secret)	spill the beans	She eventually spilt the beans. She eventually shared the secret.
E	earn (a lot)	make a killing	You could make a killing as a bookie. You could earn a lot of money taking bets.
	easy	piece-a-cake	That'd be a piece-a-cake. I'll do it with one hand behind my back. That would be very easy. I could do it without full concentration.
	enjoy	have a blast	We had a blast! We enjoyed ourselves!
E	extreme	epic	What an epic fail! What an extreme disaster!
	excited	amped	Everyone is so amped. Everyone is very excited.

F	fist fight	slug	Slug it out with skin. Fight with fists (no weapons).
	flirt	pass at	Boys don't make passes at girls who wear glasses. Boys don't flirt with girls who wear glasses.
G	government	Uncle Sam	Slinging gun for Uncle Sam. Going to war for the government.
H			
I	insult	dis	You will never dis my momma. You must not insult my mother.
	inflate (sudden price hike)	jack up	They jacked the prices right up for the Superbowl.
	infatuation	crushing	I'm crushing on Luna. I am infatuated with the Luna. I have a crush on Luna.
J			
K	killed (suddenly, esp. in an accident)	bought the farm	He bought the farm and was buried the next Tuesday. He was killed suddenly and buried the next Tuesday.
L	leave (abruptly)	bail	Why'd you bail on us? Why did you leave us (so suddenly)?
	lazy	couch potato	I want to be a couch potato this weekend. I want to be lazy this weekend.
M	money	bucks, greenbacks, scratch	You carry that kind of scratch? Do you have that much money on you?
N			
O	obese	chunky	Damn girl, you are chunky! You are really fat lady!
P	play (music)	jam	We gonna jam at Fat's tonight? Are we going to play music together at Fat's tonight?
Q	queer	homosexual	Queers, hookers and crackheads up in there. There are homosexuals, prostitutes and drug addicts there.
R	reschedule	take a raincheck	Can we take a raincheck on our dinner date? Can we reschedule out dinner date?
S	sad	blue	You're blue, what's up? You are sad, what is wrong?
	signature	John Hancock	You want my John Hancock right here? Do you want me to sign my name here?
	success	made it	You made it. You had success.
	study (last-minute after procrastinating)	cram	I'm trying to cram. I am trying to study.
T			
U	unpretentious	real, down to earth	He is so real. He is unpretentious.

V	veg	do nothing	They just want to veg out tonight. They just want to do nothing tonight.
W	weird (unpleasant)	creep/y	What a creep! What an unpleasantly weird person!
	wanting	Jonesing	I'm totally jonesing this. I really want this.
X			
Y			
Z			

UK-US English Glossary of Common Differences

Many words in UK English are the same in US English but mean entirely different things. An undershirt is a vest but a vest is a waistcoat depending on which dialect is spoken. A splashback is actually a backsplash. To solicit is to offer sex but a solicitor is a lawyer. Likewise a sleeping partner is not to be slept with but someone who for his investment can now quietly take the profit you worked hard to earn. Football is really soccer and not a game where you can touch the ball with your hands. Flannel is not a shirt but a towel for drying your body after a hot shower. The hooker has an important position on the rugby field. It is not a prostitute. You can lift a rock in America and take the lift in Britain. A dummy in Britain is for babies. An American dummy is not a real person but it is the size and shape of a real person. A shag is sexual intercourse but in the US it just refers to the type of rug. In the US a biscuit is more like a scone to a Brit. A British biscuit is more like a cookie to an American. In the US you might listen to your coach if you are training in a team sport. In the UK you would board a coach and head across country. Braces in the US straighten your teeth. Braces in the UK stop your trousers from falling. Pants in the US are really knickers in the UK. A muffler is used to silence a loud noise in the US and in the UK it means a scarf.

	UK	US
Appliances	vacuum cleaner	hoover
Building	cinder block	breeze block
	pelmet	valance
	lift	elevator
	kennel	doghouse
Clothing	trousers	pants
	braces	suspenders
	pinafore dress	jumper
	jumper	sweater
	vest	undershirt
	waistcoat	vest
	bumbag	fanny pack
Food	aubergine	eggplant
	beetroot	beets
	chips	french fries
	crisps	chips
	mangetout	snow peas
	ice lolly	popsicle
	courgette	zucchini
Games	patience	solitaire
	noughts and crosses	tic-tac-toe
Grooming	fringe	bangs
Miscellaneous items	flick knife	switchblade
	peg	clothespin
Music	crochet	quarter note
Travel	tollgate	turnpike
	petrol	gas
Vehicles	lorry	truck
	truck	18-wheeler
	bonnet	hood
	articulated lorry	trailer-tractor
	boot	trunk
	breakdown van	tow truck

Innocent words that mean something completely different to them

In Britain you may certainly "need a rubber" if you want to, for example, erase pencil markings. In America you just don't say you need a rubber to anyone. A rubber in US English is a condom.

In Britain, if your parents joined the army then you're an "army brat". It would be very rude to call anyone a "brat" in the States.

In America you can easily root for someone to win, or support them in their endeavours. In Britain, you would be taken as sleeping with them.

A fag in America is a very rude word for a homosexual man. In Britain it's only a normal word that means a cigarette. Faggot means the same in America but in Britain it just refers to an ordinary bunch of sticks needed to make a fire.

The Americans might say something is rubbish with the words "for the birds". The Brits might take that as sexist because a not particularly nice word for "ladies" to the Brits is "birds".

A pecker is a very rude word for the male sex organ in US English so if an Englishman said "keep your pecker up" or "look on the bright side" it would almost definitely be misunderstood.

Getting pissed in England means getting drunk. In America it means getting angry.

Rhyming slang

A dialect of English very specific to London is Cockney. It is often completely unintelligible, even to the British but it is also English, and very English. It is rhyming slang and usually spoken with only the first word of a phrase where the last word of the phrase rhymes with the word actually mean. Here are a small handful of examples.

Someone may say "pop up the apple for a tick". He means "run up the stairwell quickly". How would anyone know that that is what he meant? Well, the 'apple' is short for "apples and pears" and pears rhyme with stairs. Usually you won't hear the full phrase "apples and pears", they will most probably just say apples.

This kind of slang can get a little confusing. If someone says "let's take a butchers at your dog mate", he means taking a 'butcher's hook' which rhymes with look. So actually he wants to take a look at . . . your dog? No, not your dog, your dog and bone. That rhymes with phone. So what he means is he wants to take a look at your phone.

If "your Barnet's in a fuzzle" it means your hair is messy. (In this subculture the Brits don't mind making personal remarks, they find it funny. The Americans and lots of other people might find it rude.) Barnet? Barnet's fair, which rhymes with hair.

If you have ever heard of Cockney you likely know that your "trouble and strife" is your "wife". Speaking "a la mode" is speaking in "code". "Ruby for grub?" That means "Ruby Murray", or "curry".

"I'm all on me Jack Jones" means "I am all alone." Jones, alone? Well, it is not that exact a science but it does rhyme usually. Here is another example of that. Sort out the "Ave Maria" - Put out the "fire".

Ten pounds is sometimes called a "tenner" so there is no need to wonder why ten-pounds would be called an "Ayrton Senna".

Take your "AJ". That means 'take your "jacket". An "AJ" is short for "AJ Hackett". Bob's place up "ain't it a treat" means the "street".

"Spare me an able" is "give me a shilling". An "able" is short for "able and willing" which rhymes with "shilling".

"She was on the dog." It might sound fine because a "dog" or "dog and bone" is a phone. But more recently this can refer equally to crack cocaine. If you hear something like that it's hard to be sure if you should be concerned or should just wait for her to finish talking.

"Can't be sure its Adam" would mean, "can't be sure it's safe." That's because "Adam's faith" rhymes with safe, slightly. In another context it's "Adam and Eve" which rhymes with "believe". "Adam that?" means "Would you believe that?"

Took "advice from mother", did she? That means, "did she use contraceptives"? You might reply "I don't know". You would say "beats me".

Here is an abstruse one. "I kettle for ye." "Kettle" there is short for "kettle and hob". Now, you ask, how did kettle and hob come to mean watch? Kettle and hob rhymes with fob. A fob watch was used to time a boiling kettle on the stove top, or hob. So the rhyme there is a sort of double rhyme.

This rhyming slang is fairly tricky. There are hundreds of these expressions and if you have never heard it before you might take a while to catch on. For native Cockney-speakers, it's their English.

Spelling Guidelines

In US English we spell words ending in -ise with -ize as in accessorise, criticise, legitimise, traumatise or urbanise. In US English all those words would end in -ize.

The gerund from a verb ending in an -e may keep its -e and the -ing would be added in UK English. In US English the -e would fall away as is the case here where ageing and bingeing, become aging and binging. Though this is not always the case as in victimising, socialising and maximising.

Often the -re in UK English becomes a -er when written in US English such as in the words meagre and metre. In US English they would be meager and meter.

It is common for the u in UK English to disappear in US English as in mould. In US English it would be spelled mold. Baulk is British English. In American English it is balk. An even more common example is the UK English -our and the US English -or. For instance, labours, rancour and savouries in Britain are labors, rancor and savories in the States. Likewise, habour becomes habor, honour becomes honor, and flavour and favour become flavor and favor.

The double "L" in UK English usually becomes a single "L" in US English such as in dishevelled, marvellous, and woolly (US - disheveled, marvelous, wooly). But on the other hand the single "L" in UK English becomes a double "L" in US English such as in distil, fulfil and instal which would be spelled distill, fulfill and install in US English.

Not only "L" but also "G" suffers redundancy as in waggon, which in US English is wagon. The "S" faces the same fate in gasses, which becomes gases in US English.

In UK English the æ survives in words like haemorrhage and faeces. In US English that has completely disappeared. We could now correctly write hemorrhage and feces. It is similar with the word homoeopath, foetal and diarrhoea which are correctly spelled in UK English. In US English they would be correct as homeopath, fetal and diarrhea.

The -ce in UK English is often changed to -se in US English. Pretence and defence are pretense and defense. Disc in Britain is disk in America.

In almost every case -sation becomes -zation when spelled in US English. Here are a few examples idealisation, sensitisation, specialisation and organisation becomes idealization, sensitization, specialization and organization.

The -e before a suffix also disappears in US English so that judgement becomes judgment.

The French heritage of English is clear in the spellings of tonne and pouffe but the American English simplifies the spelling to ton and pouf.

The spelling may change completely between the two dialects. In UK English its gaol. In US English it is jail.

More phonetic spelling is favoured in US English as in plow, draft, sheik and pizzazz instead of plough, draught, sheikh and pzazz.

There is no rule here but the "y" in UK English often becomes another vowel in American English. Examples may be "pyjama" becoming "pajama" or "cypher" becoming "cipher". "Tyres" become "tires".

Two countries divided by a common language

You may have had a wonderful time of looking over the differences between English dialects across the Anglo-American world power. George Bernard Shaw coined a great expression describing England and America as "two countries divided by a common language". If it wasn't for TV and Internet we would probably need a UK-US English dictionary to translate from one to the other. Why not write one anyway, just for kicks . . . ?

Printed in Great Britain
by Amazon